From the Fou

SUITE
SUCCESS

RYAN WEEDEN

HOW TO MAKE **6-FIGURES** IN A SALON SUITE

Copyright © 2017 Salon Spruce Inc
MOB Founder // Spruce Owner + Master Stylist

www.mastersofbalayage.com
www.salonspruce.com

All rights reserved. No part of this book may be reproduced, stored in a retrieval system, or transmitted in any form or by any means, electronic, mechanical, photocopying, recording, or otherwise, without the prior written permission, except for inclusion of brief quotations in acknowledged reviews.

Neither the publisher nor author assumes responsibility for any accident, injuries, losses, or other damages resulting from the use of this book.

Cover: Maury Aaseng

First Edition

ACKNOWLEDGMENTS

"I'm proud of you," was all she had to say after everything I had accomplished in a seemingly short amount of time. Overcome with a sudden feeling of euphoria, it was at that moment that I realized I had reached a level of success that I had only imagined would come true many years ago. It took her words to jolt me from my common manic state that forced me to reclaim the moment and acknowledge that I had arrived.

Although it has a taken a lifetime of failures, sprinkled with various successes, it seems that the hard work and sleepless nights had begun to pay off.

I can't climb this mountain alone, and God knows I've tried. None of this would have been possible if it weren't for the love and support of my best friend and wife, Jeni. She's always there to pick me up when I'm down, remind to relax when I've piled too many projects onto my plate, and sing silly songs that we make up together after having had a few glasses of wine.

From the Earth to the Sun to the Moon and back again, you are forever my sweetheart.

I dedicate this book to my number one fan, my wife, Jeni.

I also find it necessary to offer my sincerest thanks, love and gratitude to my family for always being a solid support structure in my life. To my brother Judd, for his unbiased generosity during those dark days when I couldn't pay my phone bill. To my Mother, for her eternal optimism and faith in me (and for countless grilled cheese sandwiches when I needed a break from being an adult). To my Father, for welcoming me back home, time and time again. To my uncle Peter, my sister Mollie, to my mother-in-law Elena for helping with the edit, and for everyone else that continues to love and support me unconditionally through my journey to find my way, no matter how frustrating it must be to watch me flounder sometimes.

For all that and much more, thank you. This book is possible because of you.

"The only thing worse than starting something and failing…is not starting something."
—Seth Godin

CONTENTS

SECTION 1 — THE BIG PICTURE

WHO THIS BOOK IS FOR	8
HOW TO USE THIS BOOK	10
WHAT YOU WILL LEARN	12
THE BIG PICTURE	14

SECTION 2 — THE 7 STEPS

STEP 1 — ACT LIKE A BUSINESS — 19
   Choosing the "Right" Salon Suite
   Name Your Brand
   Create a Mobile-Friendly Website
   Establish Business Hours
   Get a Dedicated Phone Line
   Get Business Insurance

STEP 2 — EMBRACE TECHNOLOGY — 30
   Social Media
   Text Messaging
   Online Booking Systems

STEP 3 — ATTRACT YOUR PERFECT CLIENTS — 39
   The Expert Approach
   Go Greek
   Preferred Business Partnership

STEP 4 — WIN THE YELP GAME — 48
    Your Past Clients
    Your Current Clients
    Exchange Services for Reviews

STEP 5 — THE PRE-CONSULTATION — 56
    Set Yourself Up for Success

STEP 6 — THE FOLLOW-UP — 60
    Why You Should Follow Up
    How to Follow Up

STEP 7 — ASKING FOR HELP — 66
    Managing and Organization Tasks
    Maintain a High Level of Service
    Make Your Brand Appear Bigger
    Get the Truth From Follow Ups

ABOUT THE AUTHOR — 72

SECTION 1

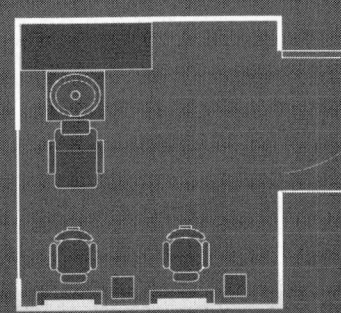

THE BIG PICTURE

"If you don't build your dream, someone
will hire you to help build theirs."
— *Tony Gaskins*

WHO THIS BOOK IS FOR

Suite Success has been created to teach winning strategies to salon suite owners. If your goal is to earn more money so that you can travel, buy nice things, have more free time, or support a family, then this book is for you.

Many stylists are choosing to open their own business in a salon suite to leave the stress and bureaucracy of large salons. This growing trend, across America, gives independent stylists the opportunity to make their own rules, be their own boss, listen to their own music, and make one hundred percent of their own earnings. This trend provides a unique opportunity for stylists to own their own business for a fraction of the cost of a traditional brick-and-mortar salon.

However, enticing as this may seem, owning your own business in a salon suite presents its own set of challenges. Although the rewards can be spectacular, succeeding in this environment does not come easy. You will have to take necessary steps to ensure that your business grows. Luckily for you, I have outlined the seven steps you must take in order to turn your new business into a money-making machine.

These proven techniques have been carefully designed and practiced throughout my own business. Consistent application of the seven steps took my business from earning less than $1,200 per month, to over $15,000 per month, in less than two years.

So why should I give you my secrets? It's my belief that every one of us that strives to succeed, deserves to succeed. But life is tough. It's not enough to work hard anymore. It's about working smarter and learning from other people's mistakes. It's about sharing our knowledge to help each other grow. With more competition in the world than ever before, I feel it's my duty to help you succeed, as others have done for me. Let's unite, inspire one another, and share in each others victories.

This book consists of seven, simple steps. Follow them in order and don't skip any. With consistent application, your business will undoubtedly grow at an exponential rate.

HOW TO USE THIS BOOK

Let's imagine, for a second, that you're trying to put together a bedroom dresser, piece by piece. You open the box and lay everything out on the floor. As you look through the package, you see more than a dozen wooden planks, two bags full of screws with washers to match, a dozen plastic inserts, a handful of nails, some zip-tie looking gadget, and an Allen wrench. Might you dare try to put this beast together without using the seven page instruction manual that it came with? I wouldn't. You would be wise to follow the directions of assembly if you wish your dresser to function properly. I guarantee that if you decide to "wing it", you'll end up with a bunch of extra pieces and furniture that could fall apart at any second. Skipping a step in the instructions can also lead to total failure, as each step builds on one another in order to guarantee a successful outcome.

The same can be said for opening your salon suite. Just "winging it" is not a good idea. Although you don't need to have a well thought out business plan (I didn't have one), you do need to realize that you are stepping into the world of business ownership. Things are different now.

During my time in the salon suites, I have seen dozens of aspiring stylists, estheticians, nail techs, and massage therapists come and go. Over and over again, I've been witness to these over-zealous suite owners setting up their businesses without any backbone. Without structure or support. Without a plan. It's no surprise that one day they are here and the next day, gone.

Watching a starry-eyed entrepreneur get crushed by the throws of reality is never something I like to see. I've been there and wouldn't wish the pain of business failure on anyone.

In the earlier example, you were using the given instructions to build a bedroom dresser as it was designed. Following these steps would assure you that the completed product would function as intended. Each step is designed to be followed, in order, so that you will reach a successful outcome. In this case, a dresser.

Building a business is no different. There are steps you need to take in order to reach a high level of success. If you want to earn 100K a year, you need a plan.

In Section Two, you'll get to the seven steps. This is your instruction manual. Read it carefully and don't skip anything. The seven steps in this book are ordered in such a way that they can be approached, literally, step-by-step. One chapter follows the next and builds upon the principles before.

I'd recommend reading the book all the way through first, earmarking pages you want to come back to. Then, once you've finished, revisit those areas of focus where your business needs attention the most.

The steps in this book will build the foundation of your business. Practice the strategies laid out before you with vigor and consistency and you will have a wealth- building salon suite.

WHAT YOU WILL LEARN

This book will not teach you how to cut and color hair. That's up to you. Today, there are more than enough YouTube tutorials, Instagram videos, and professional training academies across the world that can teach you the technical skills of cutting and coloring hair.

What this book will teach you is how to quickly start a business from scratch and make it massively successful in only a matter of months.

As you read the chapters you will learn not only how to survive on your own, but how to thrive on your own. I will show you ways to break through the barriers of what you thought was possible, and you don't have to be a Celebrity Stylist to do it.

You will learn how to quickly develop your brand, attract the perfect clientele, build a five star reputation, and make more money than you ever thought possible, all on a shoestring budget.

I'm certain you will find that this short, yet powerful handbook, is a necessary ally in helping you to create the salon business of your dreams. You'll see that the potential is only limited to what you believe is possible.

I believe that anyone that strives to be successful, deserves to be successful. There are enough people on the planet with enough hair to go around. We are all in this together so let's share in each other's successes and benefit from our epiphanies. As they say, sharing is caring.

Remember, I have done the hard work for you. I have spent thousands of dollars on countless marketing strategies to discover what works and what doesn't. For two years, I barely slept as I was creating this wonderful, winning business model that I now offer to you. Please take it, use it, and profit from it. Then share it.

THE BIG PICTURE

> "Sometimes in the waves of change
> we find our true direction."
> — *Anonymous*

Being a hairstylist is a worthless profession and you can't make a living at it. At least that's what someone told me. Someone I loved, trusted and cared about deeply. So I believed her.

At the time, I had just started working at a new salon, in a new area, so of course I wasn't making any money yet. I could barely afford my car payment. How could I ever support a family?

I was ashamed of myself, but only because someone else told me that I should be.

That's when I quit the business altogether, after five years of working in reputable salons. Although I was becoming a very talented hairstylist, I couldn't see the big picture.

That's when I decided to grow up, so-to-speak, and join adulthood, the land of responsibility. I took an entry-level job at a large corporation, and moved into my new home, a 5x5 cubicle. I hated it almost immediately but figured that was just part of having a so-called "real" job. I'd wake up before the sun rose, sit in traffic drinking my hot coffee, inching along with the rest of corporate America, just so I could get to work ready to answer phones and type emails by 8:00a.m. At the end of day, around 5:30–6:00 p.m., I'd hurriedly straightened the papers scattered across my desk, race to my car, jump back into traffic, and pray that I'd get home by dark. I now understood what working for the weekend meant. Friday couldn't come fast enough.

Within a few months I felt like I was drowning. Neither my heart nor my mind belonged in that type of environment. My smile faded and depression set in. I had become a 9:00–5:00 p.m. drone, which in actuality is more like 8:00–6:00 p.m. I was always on somebody else's schedule and my email inbox was dictating my life.

After less than just two years, I was "let go", which is a nice way to say I was fired. My sales numbers weren't hitting the mark and my progress had slowed considerably from when I had first started.

None of this was a shock to me because I didn't care. I absolutely hated every moment of every day. You know that line in the movie "Office Space", where the lead character confesses to his therapist that because of his job, he felt that every day was the worst day of his life? That about summed it up for me.

When I got home from my last day, I was overwhelmed with a sense of relief. I knew that this type of job would never satisfy me, so I crossed it off the list.

However, still convinced I needed a "real job", I decided to become a real estate agent. I could make my own schedule, be my own boss, and control my own fate. I admired the independence and could work from anywhere. No more cubicles. Also, after watching a series of real estate reality shows, I was aware of the kind of money that was possible to be made.

This was a pivotal point in my life. Not because I was good at real estate. I wasn't. I was a terrible real estate agent. I didn't know anything about houses and frankly, I didn't care. The reason this choice became so vital was because I was able to meet someone that I never would have crossed paths with if I hadn't decided to give real estate a shot.

This person became my friend, my teacher, and my mentor. He taught me skills that were so valuable, so limitless, that they could be applied to any field, not just real estate. My mind was opening to a new way of seeing the world and my place in it.

His gift to me was a rekindling of my own passion and spirit. I found myself dreaming again. Finally, I was able to view my passion of being a hairstylist, with a brand-new set of eyes. More purposeful eyes.

I could now see the Big Picture.

It was time to say goodbye to "real jobs" and begin to follow my heart, my soul, and my spirit.

It wasn't about a label anymore. I wasn't going to be just a hair stylist. I was a visionary. I was an entrepreneur, an artist and creator. I was whatever I wanted to be.

Doing hair wasn't going to be a job anymore. It was now a vehicle, a transport, a way to take me to that extraordinary life I had always dreamed of living. *Hair* can take me there, I realized.

It had been over three years since I had picked up a pair of scissors or put foils in someone's hair. I couldn't believe I was about to find myself back in the hair business.

When I first got back behind the chair, I was starving for business. With less than ten clients in my book, I was barely making $500 a month. Thankfully, my loving parents were letting me crash on a blowup futon on the floor of the dining room.

I knew it wouldn't be for long, though, because now I had a plan. With my mind clear, thanks to my mentor, I started developing strategies that I would use to hopefully boost my business, strengthen my reputation, and earn more money than I had ever thought possible. I was training myself to think outside the box, with a bigger picture in mind of what was realistically possible in the scope of most hairstylists' visions.

Now, just three years later, my personal income has skyrocketed to nearly $17,000 a month—over $200K a year. My business is better than ever and I have a three month waiting list for new clients. My salon is ranked one of the highest-rated in all of San Diego, and it's only a salon suite. This success was more than I had ever dreamed of just a few years prior.

My personal life was also thriving. In that same span of three years, as I was tenaciously developing myself as an independent stylist, I was fortunate enough to marry the love of my life, get a house by the beach, and start a family.

Not only did these strategies help me succeed in business, they also helped me succeed in my personal life. It was the most satisfying feeling to realize I finally had found the perfect work/life balance.

Thinking back, it was foolish of me for believing those hurtful words, "being a hairstylist isn't good enough". It's complete rubbish. Being a hairstylist can be whatever you want it to be.

As you continue to read, I want you to think of yourself as more than just a hairstylist. I want you to start seeing your own *Big Picture*.

SECTION 2

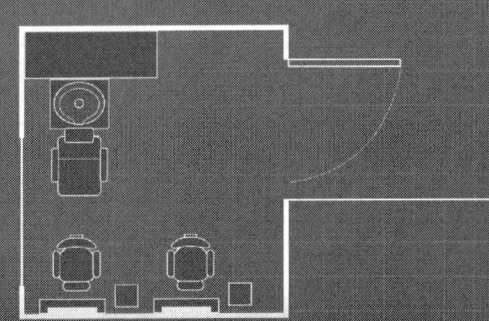

THE 7 STEPS

"The best way to predict the future is to create it."
—*Stephen Covey*

STEP 1 — ACT LIKE A BUSINESS

> "As you think, so shall you become."
> —*Bruce Lee*

You have decided to have your own business and be your own boss. Bravo!

But what does that mean exactly?

I'll tell you. It means you need to think bigger than yourself. You're not just *you* anymore. You are now your *business*. Although you are the talent and probably the *only* employee in your new venture, you still need to "Act Like a Business". Even if you are your own one-man army, a solopreneur, it's time to think *beyond* yourself and expand the range of your thought.

Here's the scary part. You are now responsible for your own brand. No longer can you hide under the roof of someone else's salon and complain that certain things aren't the way *you* would have it if it was *your* salon. From the very first contact you have with potential customers, all the way to the end of their experience, it is your responsibility. A customer experience needs to flow, be stress-free, and exciting.

It's your business now, and the experience you are providing is under your control and your control only.

I've heard women say before that it's harder to leave their hairdresser than it is to leave their partner. I realize that there's a bit of humor at play in that statement, but I also think there's a lot of truth to it as well. Men and women love their stylists, and I'm sure they will love you too. But they have to find you first, so focus on impressing them from the start.

When new clients find you, they need to be impressed. Blown away even. Have you ever online dated or known someone that has? Well, having your salon stand out amongst the crowd is really not that much different. As online daters are scrolling for possible "mates", potential salon clients are undoubtedly seeking love as well, except in this case, it's for their hair. In both cases, you are absolutely inundated with possibilities. Many can be written off right away, because in one way or another the person (or salon) has failed to grab your attention and meet your personal criteria. So you continue to swipe or click to find the right match. The ones that do manage to catch your attention, probably do so within a fraction of a second. Something about the person (or salon) was attractive to you in one way or another.

What was it that grabbed your attention? If you haven't done this search for yourself, do it now. Pretend you are you looking for a salon professional to cut or color *your* hair.

Right now, do a quick search on Google or Yelp for salons in your area that could potentially fit your own personal hair needs. See what pops up. Which ones catch your attention and why? Is it something as simple as their fancy name or something more complex like a well-designed website? Whatever it is, take a minute and write it down.

Now go back and preview several of the salons that you'd never set foot in. Why do you immediately vote them out? What is it specifically that turns you off? Is it the low star rating and customer complaints? Maybe it's their cheesy website and lack of professionalism? Again, take a minute and jot down a few notes. Referring back to these when you are setting up your business (or updating it) is highly valuable. Your potential clients are going to be doing the same search and thinking about the same things. Think about what kind of first impression you want to make.

Your brand needs to be impressive, confident and professional. Potential customers need to feel like they know you, like you, and trust you, before they even contact you.

Ask yourself why someone would choose you over the dozens of competitors in your market area. Is it your killer personality? Ha!

No. They need to meet you first. Your personality comes into play later, to keep them coming back.

First impressions are everything and your first impression needs to be killer. Your name, reputation, and business branding need to be attractive for your target audience.

Having an entire brand can be time-consuming and expensive. But it doesn't have to be. It can be done for pennies on the dollar. When I first started out I was broke. I had to save money and cut financial corners in every possible way.

In the sections ahead, I've highlighted some key areas to focus on to help you create a competition-crushing first impression.

CHOOSING THE "RIGHT" SALON SUITE

When you've finally decided to make the jump to your own salon suite, there are a lot of factors to consider. Above all else, this is the most important decision you can make. You are looking for a new place to call home, a place where your clients will be excited to be, and something that will be enticing to new clients coming through the door. Don't choose something based primarily on price. Just because something may be a good deal, doesn't mean it's right for you. Here are some key factors to consider when picking your new salon.

1. Location, Location, Location. Just as they say in real estate, the same can be said for where you operate your business. Location is very important. Most salon suite environments don't have much visibility from the street. The name of the building might be evident, such as Phenix Salon Suites or Sola Salons for example, but your particular business probably won't have any signage, unless you're in the very front in some cases.

In choosing your salon suite location, here are some good questions to ask yourself which will help zero you on the right space.

- Will I be happy here for a few years?
- Will my ideal clientele feel comfortable here?
- Is it easy to get to?
- Is this area the vibe I'm going for?

Take some time to answer those questions, and you will soon determine which areas will best suit you and your business.

2. Parking. The first salon I ever booth rented from was in downtown San Diego. The space itself was awesome, but the parking was practically non-existent. The only option my clients had was limited, metered street parking. Worse than that, these paid meters were only good for two hours, which meant that any service that ran over two hours, required either myself or my client running out, embarrassingly in public, to add more quarters. Because I believe in always delivering the best in customer service, I wouldn't dream of asking my clients to run out into public, full of foils and hair color, to feed a meter.

This routine got old pretty quickly. Plus, I ended up spending a lot of my own money paying for their parking. I was already charging a lot for their service, so tacking on an additional two to three dollars was pretty low, in my opinion.

Many salon suites will have parking nearby, unless it's in a busy downtown area, like mine is now. My suites are currently located in downtown La Jolla, a busy part of town—very touristy—with tricky, two-hour parking. Thankfully, one of the perks I got for renting this particular suite, was garage parking. By only paying a small additional fee each month, I'm able to validate all of the clients' parking for free, no restrictions. It's half a block from my salon and couldn't be better.

When weighing your options, be sure to choose a salon suite that makes customer parking easy. No one likes to drive around and around hoping for something to open up. Make sure your clients can find parking quickly and easily.

3. Deciding on Lease Terms. One of the best things about starting out in a salon suite is that you typically don't have to sign a standard three to five year lease. Many are month to month. Others may be a year or two in the case of tenant improvements—such as knocking down a wall and increasing the salon space at the landlord's expense.

Since owning a salon may not be the right fit for everyone, be sure to choose a salon suite that doesn't commit you to a long term of financial responsibility. If your business fails or you hate the salon suite life, you can cut your losses quickly and move on. You can't do that if you're stuck in a three to five year lease.

NAME YOUR BRAND

In thinking beyond yourself, you need to think *bigger* than yourself. When you first start off you might have business cards that say "Hair by Jess." That's okay to start, but now it's time for you to open the door to future possibilities and begin building a brand that your loyal followers can stand behind.

People love brands. Think Nike, Nordstrom, Starbucks, and Amazon to name a few. All these brands represent something big and special. You may not like some of them, but I'm sure you're aware that many people do. That's because they've built brand loyalty.

They are loyal to their brand. They trust it. They respect it.

Lululemon didn't invent the yoga pant, but you'd sure think they did. Women identify with this brand because they love it, trust it, and appreciate the quality.

That's what your brand needs to reflect. Love, trust and quality.

Yes, the brands I listed above are giants, and most of our businesses will never even come close to competing on that level. That's not what I'm talking about. I'm simply inviting you to expand your mind a little bit.

If your business card says "Hair by Jess", you are selling yourself short. It comes across as small and unimaginative. It tells the world that you have arrived and that there is nowhere else for you to go. Do you really want to portray that?

Don't take this personally, as that's not my intention. A name like "Hair by Jess", for example, has the potential to be super successful, as does any other business. But in order to grow, you need a brand. Something bigger than yourself that your supporters can fully get behind. They already love you, so why not invite them to take an active role toward helping you succeed in a larger goal. I can't imagine you want to be a hairdresser at age eighty, do you? Something needs to give. Start tapping into your potential now.

I get asked all the time why (and how) I came up with the name *Salon Spruce*. I tell them it's because I envisioned a future. I wasn't sure what it was—sure, I'd been working on hair solo for awhile—but I imagined something *bigger* than myself. What if in a few years I decided to open a bigger place, and hire some employees? I couldn't imagine anyone wanting to work for a salon called *Hair by Ryan*.

Additionally, if I decide to open a bigger salon someday, I will carry my brand reputation with me, and my clients will undoubtedly follow. They are faithful to my Spruce brand and culture and couldn't imagine a life without it.

You might be thinking that you can always come up with a business name if and when you decide to expand, right? Of course you can! But why wait? Did you know it takes years to build brand loyalty? It took me three years of hard work to become the highest rated salon in my city. So the sooner you start branding your business, the better.

The best time to start developing your brand is when you first go into business for yourself. Not only will you probably have more time to focus on branding (when you don't have a full clientele and employees to manage), your brand will grow as you do. This gives you the opportunity to continually fine tune it along the way to create the perfect brand experience for your customers.

My salon (and brand), Salon Spruce, is the culmination of years of trial and error. From my first days of booth-renting to my current salon, my brand continues to evolve as I do. As I mature in my craft, my business matures, and maturity equals success. I have learned what works and what doesn't. And because you're reading this, you get to benefit too. You don't have to make the same mistakes I did. You can skip ahead, make the right decisions, and move forward at an exponential rate. Just read, listen, and act. That's all. You'll learn what works and what doesn't in your own market area, but regardless, you will be ahead of the game, as you apply these essential principles toward your own success.

As you create a brand, you are creating an experience for your clients. Make it special. Be proud of your business and its potential.

Don't wait until you have your "ideal" place or your "dream" salon. Start building it now.

CREATE A MOBILE-FRIENDLY WEBSITE

You need a website for your business, but of course you already knew that. However, at first, I'd recommend staying far away from professional web designers, unless you have a lot of money to burn. Hiring a professional will cost you thousands of dollars before your website is even up and running. Website builders will try to convince you that you need a slew of extras and add-ons that your small business can clearly do without at first. It's like going to get your oil changed for $19. By the time you leave, you've spent nearly $60 because they've up-sold you on everything from a new air filter to super-premium oil.

If I'm to guess, I'd say you are probably at the beginning stages of opening (or expanding) your small business, right? I'm also guessing you have a very small budget. I know I did. So let's be extra cost-conscious at these early stages.

I researched the cost of having a professional to create my own website. When the number I was quoted was more than I was making, I decided to figure out how to build it myself. Then one day, when I could afford to pay someone to do it, is when I would hand off the baton. I started reading books and learning web design. This was seven years ago in early 2010. Website creation at that time was complicated, but being a technologically savvy man, I figured it out after countless hours of trial and error.

When I started writing this book last year, I researched what it would take to develop a website today, in 2017. To my delight, I was amazed to see how absolutely far website design has come. Not only do you *not* have to hire someone to do it for you, you don't even have to understand website coding. It's all simple "drag and drop". Easier than creating a MySpace page, when that was a thing.

Companies like Wordpress, 1and1.com, Wix, and Squarespace, help you set up and create your own customized website in minutes. No longer do we need to recruit a web designer to develop your site. Today, anyone can spend a couple of hours and have a professionally attractive, functional website. And that's all you need right now.

I was able to create my salon website, all on my own, for only $50. It was up-and- running in 24-hours. The best part is that I can update whenever I like without having to call a so-called specialist.

ESTABLISH BUSINESS HOURS

When you work for yourself, it's tricky separating your work life from your personal life, but it is possible. One thing that helps significantly, is establishing your hours of operation.

Your business hours are the days and times your business officially opens and closes during the week. Once you decide which days you intend to be open, make sure the hours are displayed everywhere. On your website, booking site, Yelp page, Google listing, and on your voicemail. I guarantee, you'll be less likely to receive those 11:00 p.m. client phone calls asking to schedule a hair appointment for the next morning.

Choose your "open" hours. Let's say it's Tuesday through Saturday from 10:00–7:00 p.m. Only answer the phone, text, and email clients during those business hours. If someone calls at 7:30 p.m., let it go to voicemail. If it's urgent, you can call them back. But if it's not, and it probably isn't, you can return the message tomorrow, during your next "business" day. Just because we all have cell phones now doesn't mean it's our responsibility to be available 24–7.

Once you let customers know they can reach you after hours, you can expect them to always contact you, after hours. Do you really want your phone buzzing at 11:30 p.m.? Because it will, trust me. You need to set your boundaries early on.

Remember, you are a business now. Act like one.

GET A DEDICATED PHONE LINE

The best way to personally adhere to your business hours is to have a separate salon phone line. You don't necessarily need to have a separate phone, but it can help significantly.

1. Add a line to your cellular plan. This is what we did and it's been a sanity saver. We simply added a cell phone to our "family" plan and paid for a basic phone, which was free. So, for $38 per month (which is a business write-off) we can now ensure that our business hours stay business hours.

Here's another bonus. With our *Spruce* phone, we are sure to always answer professionally, because anyone calling could be a customer. We are also able to create a professional voicemail greeting that lets people know our hours, special events, and anything else that might be helpful for them to know. Best part of all, after we close shop for the day, we can put it on silent. No more late night client calls, ever.

2. Get a "Google Voice" Number. Have you heard of Google Voice? If not, check it out. It's amazing. I used this tool when I first began booth renting as a way of separating my business life from my personal life. For those of you that aren't familiar with it, Google Voice is a tool provided by Google that allows you to create an additional phone number for the phone you already use. This second phone number will then be set to forward calls to your personal phone.

The reasons for doing this are simple. Within the Google Voice settings, you can set times of the day that your number will actively forward calls. Let's say it's Tuesday and your business hours are 10:00–6:00 p.m. You can set these hours in Google Voice for forwarding to your cell phone. Before or after hours, callers will go straight to a second voicemail that you can set up in the Google Voice settings.

You can even receive and respond to text messages through the Google application.

If you're not ready to invest in a separate phone line, I highly recommend starting with Google Voice. It's free and gets the job done. Then, one day down the road, when you're overwhelmingly busy, invest in a separate phone. Your sanity will thank you for it.

GET BUSINESS INSURANCE

In recent years, a woman almost died by having her hair shampooed. You may be rolling your eyes and think I'm crazy, but I'm not. Go look it up. In 2013, at a salon in San Diego, a forty-eight year old woman was getting her hair shampooed. Nothing out of the ordinary. However, less than two weeks later she suffered a massive stroke and nearly died. Doctors were able to tie the stroke to the impact on her neck from the cramped shampoo bowl. Beauty Parlor Stroke Syndrome, they called it. Yes, it's a thing. It's a rare occurrence but has been documented as a possible side effect to simply getting your head washed at a salon.

You better believe there was a lawsuit involving the salon.

Did you know that each year there are over twenty-million lawsuits in the United States? We live in a society that loves quick money and some people are willing to sue anyone for anything just to line their pocketbooks. To protect yourself, you need to get some decent business insurance.

I realize the story I just told you may seem a little far-fetched. Let me give you one more example. Something you may have even come close to doing on your own. This next story happened to me just a few months ago.

One of my regulars came in for a routine haircut. He'd been in probably about twenty times over the last two years. I was an ace with his hair and could almost do it blindfolded. But on this particular day I was more stressed out than usual. There was a lot on my mind and I was more distracted than usual. I was concerned about bills I had to pay, phone calls I had to make, and clients I had forgotten to schedule. My mental "to do" list was going crazy. To top it off, I was running thirty minutes late. At any moment my next client would be walking through the door and I was glancing over my shoulder in anticipation.

That's when it happened. As I was scissor-over-combing just behind his right ear, my freshly sharpened blades sliced through the tip of his ear like butter, nearly snipping it off entirely. My client yelped in pain and reached for his ear. I instantly turned white with shock and watched the blood pour from the fresh laceration. I quickly grabbed a towel and applied pressure on it. The tip of his ear was barely hanging on.

All I could think was how glad I was to have insurance to protect me from such mishaps.

That'll never happen to you, you might think. That's what I thought, too. But it did happen and it *does* happen. Thankfully, he *did* like me and understood that I simply had a bad day. I gladly paid his doctor's bill to get his ear stitched up and offered him free haircuts for the rest of the year. That's the least I could do for someone being so understanding. The way I see it, I got off easy.

Thankfully, my client was not out to ruin me or my business by filing a huge lawsuit. He appreciated the great work I had always done. He said mistakes of that nature rarely befall someone with as much focus and talent that I have always provided. I was grateful for his supportive statement. It reassured me as a professional as I was feeling pretty low in that instance.

Unfortunately, not everyone is so understanding. If this had happened to a new client, I'm certain I would have been sued for damages. That's why you need to be protected.

I'm sure your clients love you to death, but that doesn't mean they won't sue you for damages if you happened to spill bleach in their eye. Bottom line, get insurance. This is to protect you and your business from any unfortunate accidents. Now go make a few calls and secure some insurance.

STEP 2 — EMBRACE TECHNOLOGY

"Life is Change. Growth is optional. Choose wisely."
—*Karen Kaiser Clark*

If you're not using technology to help your business, it's time to sit down and figure it out.

I don't care if you've been doing hair for two months or twenty years, the same rules apply. You need clients in your chair to make money. And, in order to get new clients, you need to attract new business, right?

As the world gets crazier and more complicated, it's important for us to simplify the salon experience for our clients as much as possible. We can do this by utilizing the latest and greatest technology to our advantage.

Technology provides us with so many options that deciding which tools will best suit our business growth can be overwhelming. To help you cut through the clutter, I'm recommending a few key areas where I think you should focus your time.

SOCIAL MEDIA

I know you don't live in a cave and that you've heard of Facebook, Instagram, Twitter and other cleverly named apps. But are you using them?

Social media platforms such as Facebook, Instagram, YouTube, and Pinterest are great for connecting your business to both current and prospective clients. With careful planning and consistent engagement, it's possible to attract new clients, connect with existing clients, and market your business for free. Free is good. We like free.

The Internet is here to stay. It's time you learn how to use it. Better yet, master it. If you want to be earning six-figures per year, it's imperative that you're on social media. There's no better way to showcase your work, attract new business, and promote your professional services. And again, it's free.

In the beginning stages of building your business, you really only need to focus on three platforms.

1. Instagram. This popular app can be quickly downloaded to your phone (for free). It has quickly become a very huge asset within the hair industry. It is being used by hair artists to showcase the great work they do, as well as by potential customers who are seeking talented stylists. If your work is well represented on Instagram, you can attract business clients and reap the reward of free marketing.

Here are some quick pointers to help your work stand out amongst the competition.

Take a good photo. This is easier said than done. Sometimes your exceptional hair styling doesn't transfer to a photo. Don't let this discourage you. It happens to all of us, regardless of our skill level. Sometimes the hair is awesome and the photo is dismal, no matter what angle you shoot it from.

With practice, your photos will get better and better and soon you will be churning out one incredible image after another. You can utilize various techniques such as:

- Different cameras
- Multiple lenses
- Photo backdrops
- Switching the angle of the photo
- Playing with lighting
- Adjusting the poses

Try everything until you find out what works best for you and the space you're working in. Take as many photos as you can until you find that sweet spot.

Do not filter or photoshop your photos heavily. Small enhancements are fine, but altering the photo drastically is a complete misrepresentation of your work. Don't lie to yourself, your peers, or your potential customers. Focus on creating exceptional work and taking great photos.

Post your work often. Most stylists don't post their work enough. In order to generate buzz, you need to be engaging the public regularly. The goal of regular posting is to attract people to "follow you" and subscribe to your content.

It's equally important that your content stays relevant. If your intention is to promote yourself as a fantastic stylist, then showcasing photos of your puppy are not in your best interest. Although adding photos of your personal life help you come across as more personable, keep your content strictly professional. If you still want to share photos of your spouse or other loved ones, do so on a personal page.

If you're new to Instagram and other social media platforms, you probably don't have much content to post yet. I'd recommend posting work from other hair artists you admire and label them as "inspiration photos". Don't forget to give credit to the artist or you'll come off as an imposter.

Ask your clients to "tag" you in selfies. When your clients leave the salon they are feeling good about themselves. You undoubtedly gave them a remarkable service and they are smitten. It's a good hair day in their book. Chances are that sometime in the next day or two, your client will want to snap a photo and post it somewhere on social media.

This is your opportunity for free marketing. I'm religious about asking my clients at the end of their service to please tag me in any good hair photos they take. By asking, I'm planting the seed for them to take action, and in essence, do me a favor. It also ensures that they will take a good photo so as to not offend their hairdresser.

Asking your client to tag you in a photo may seem like a small favor to them, but it's a huge marketing play for you. Consumers would rather receive a recommendation from a friend (even via social media), than get bombarded by ads from a business that's forcefully promoted.

Never underestimate the power of the client selfie. It's free marketing and all you have to do is ask.

Learn How To Use Hashtags. Hashtags are a way to create a searchable link. For instance, if you want to search "balayage", type in "#balayage". If you post a photo of balayage that you've done, type "#balayage" into the comment section of Instagram or Facebook. Anyone that types in the search keyword "#balayage" will have a chance to see your work. Be sure that when you type in the hashtag, to leave out the quotations.

So why is this important?

It's another free marketing tool to help get you discovered by potential clients in your area.

More and more people are using hashtags to search popular items everyday. You can use them on Google, Facebook, Twitter, Instagram, and a number of other search engines.

Let me teach you how it works by explaining how we use it to boost our own business's visibility. My personal specialty is balayage which makes my ideal client anyone that wants balayage. I'll post a photo of my recent balayage work on Instagram (for example), and then add in my hashtags. My goal with my hashtags is to reach anyone that is searching for a balayage specialist in and around La Jolla/San Diego—where my salon is located.

For example, in my own business, I may post hashtags like this: #sandiegobalayage #lajollabalayage #lajollahairsalon #lajollahairstylist #sandiegohairstylist #lajollasalon #sandiegosalon *etc., etc.*

Please note that in order for these to work properly, all hashtags must be followed by at least one word or phrase with no spaces. This means that a hashtag like "#sandiegobalayage" would work, but "#san diego balayage" wouldn't. The search engines would only read "#san" in the latter example, so make sure that no spaces exist within the search phrase you are using.

Furthermore, Instagram allows you to use a maximum of thirty hashtags with every post. I recommend you use all thirty for maximum searchability.

To save time, I jot down the thirty hashtags I use the most and put them into my *Notes* section on my phone. Then, each time I post something, to save me the time and monotony of trying to remember all thirty hashtags, I copy and paste. Done and done.

Want more Instagram Advice? Go to our website: www.mastersofbalayage.com/downloadsand download *The Top 10 Steps to the Perfect Instagram Post*.

2. Facebook. With nearly 1.7 billion monthly users, Facebook is one of the largest online "Show and Tell" sites in history. Although you may be more into Snapchat or Instagram (or whatever the new, current thing is at the moment), that doesn't mean you should ignore it. This isn't about you anymore, it's about your business, and your business needs to have its own existence. You may have your own page, but now your business (your brand) needs one, too. Set up a page and schedule a little bit of time to update it every week. Add new content, photos, and interesting article links. Just like Instagram, you want to add new content often.

Once you have enough worthwhile content, you'll inevitably have people that start responding to your posts. Be sure to communicate with them, professionally, even if you just "like" their comment. People love to be heard online or they wouldn't take the time to comment. By responding promptly to people's comments and messages, you show that you care. People like that, and in turn, will engage in your posts more frequently.

3. YouTube. Videos are the future. No question about it. According to Cisco, by the year 2017, video will account for 69% of all consumer internet traffic. So what does this mean to you? It's time to stop being camera shy and get in front of the camera instead of always behind it. It's true that people fear public speaking more than they fear death—which is odd—but I guess it makes sense. When you're dead, there's no chance of facing rejection or embarrassment. That's not to say that you might wish you were dead the first few times you see yourself on camera. Don't worry, though, you'll get better and better as you practice. Practice and practice more.

So what are your videos going to be about? Think of it as another way to showcase your work and your professional style. For example, my videos are instructional by nature. My passion is educating other stylists, so I purpose my videos to do just that. I offer up advice on what I've learned along the way, which may help them to do the same. Sometimes I feel like I'm simply speaking to a younger me. I want that younger me to succeed, and to do so without making the same mistakes I made. It's like all that advice you never took from your parents, but wish you did. That's how I go about my videos.

For you, your goal may be to attract new clients. Great! You need to showcase the great work you do for all to see. So go set up a video camera near your styling chair and press record. Just make sure you ask your client's permission first or they may think you're a creeper.

Another excellent way to build your confidence and comfort in front of the camera is to demonstrate your skills on a mannequin head. You don't even have to speak. Just demonstrate what you are doing while the camera is rolling. Look at someone brilliant like @confessionsofahairstylist or @heatherchapman. By the way, those are their Instagram handles. Oftentimes, they only use mannequin heads to show different techniques. During the editing phase, insert upbeat background music and voila, you have a video! Now post it and create another.

TEXT MESSAGING

It seems that no one wants to talk on the phone anymore. True. But in my experience, when it comes to scheduling appointments and communicating with your clients, that's a good thing! Here are a few reasons why teaching your clients to text you is a win-win for all parties involved.

1. Faster client response. People respond quicker to text messages than to voicemails. Why? Because it's easier.

2. You don't need to respond immediately. That's not to say you wait two days before getting back to someone. However, when somebody calls, they expect someone to pick up the phone. They want something now and are not interested in leaving a voicemail.

3. There is no question about what is written. Say a client walks into your salon today at 10:00 a.m. for her appointment. She's excited and ready to get her hair done. The problem is, you weren't expecting her until 10:00 a.m. *next* week on the same day. Who made the mistake? The text will tell you. If it's you—shame on you—then you can begin your heartfelt apology. If it's her, I'm sure she'll be extremely embarrassed but won't hold any blame on you. She'll apologize, and come back next week.

4. It's easy to confirm your appointments and follow up with clients. Whether you are confirming your clients for the week—which we always do—or following up with your clients after a service, texting makes it easy. On Saturdays of each week, we make it a point to confirm ALL of our appointments for the following week. Although your clients may not like having their weekend interrupted by a phone call from you—which would probably go straight to voicemail—they don't mind a quick text reminding them about their upcoming visit. This is what we send:

"Hi (insert client name),
Just confirming your upcoming hair appointment for (insert date
*   and time). Please reply YES to confirm. Thank you,*
(insert your name)"

Easy, right? And who would that annoy? No one. Nine times out of ten, we'll get a response by the end of the day. Most clients will confirm with a "YES" and others—who may have completely forgotten about the appointment—will ask to reschedule. That's fine. It's better than a no-show. Since making this policy customary,

I've had less than ten no-shows over the last four years. I'd say that's a pretty low number because I typically have more than seventy clients in my chair per month.

The same goes for following up with your clients after a service. I will dive into that a little deeper in the chapter "The Follow Up".

Texting is the most widely used form of communication in the world today. There is now an emerging disease linked to "over-texting" called De Quervain tenosynovitis. Thankfully, it's not contagious or deadly. Just tricky to pronounce.

The point is this, the whole world is texting, so why are you trying to conduct business without it?

My salon offers text communication with our clients regarding almost everything. 95% of our client communication is done with texting. We schedule and confirm appointments, check in with clients, conduct simple consultations and notify clients if our stylists are running behind. Just be sure you go into your settings and disable the "Read Now" notification alert. That's a Pro-Tip, for you. Once your clients see you've read their message, they'll expect a response promptly. We all know how it feels to be ignored.

Before I end this section, let me leave you with a few quick tips regarding text messaging:

- Messages can be easily misinterpreted. Always sound thankful and excited. Use exclamations ("!") and smileys (":)") more than you would in real life.
- Use correct grammar. Remember, you're a *business* not a teenager. You need to reflect professionalism. Act like a grownup.
- Be prompt in your responses. Returning texts two days later is amateurish and lackadaisical.

ONLINE BOOKING SYSTEMS

One of the most beneficial apps available to salon owners is for their clients to have the ability to book online, at their own convenience.

Research suggests, due to our ever-increasing busy schedules, a large majority of clients prefer to do their appointment bookings early in the morning or very late at night, before or after business hours.

Why is this?

It's because people are working longer hours than ever before and have a myriad of more work to do during the day, where lunch hours are short and hurried, if they're lucky enough to get a lunch at all. The only available time many working professionals have to schedule anything is long after regular business hours end.

Allowing potential clients the option to book their appointments online makes the scheduling experience with you easy, professional, and convenient.

Better yet, you don't have to lift a finger.

Many independent stylists and salon suite owners I've spoken with use simple and cost-effective services like *Styleseat.com* or *Schedulicity.com* while others use more robust systems like *MindBody.com*, *Booker.com*, or *Vagaro*.

Over the years I've used several of these systems and I've noticed that each version has its advantages and disadvantages. The cheaper ones (some are free), offer online booking but not many bells and whistles, such as financial income reporting and employee performance tracking. The more robust systems—the ones that do have all the extras—cost you a pretty penny each month.

Determining which one is the best fit for your business might take a little research.

No matter which route you decide to take, offering online booking to your clients is invaluable. Soon your phone will be dinging with new appointments.

STEP 3—ATTRACT YOUR PERFECT CLIENTS

> "He who is not courageous enough to take
> risks will accomplish nothing in life."
> —Muhammad Ali

What is the perfect client? You ask a dozen people and you will probably get a dozen different answers. Some stylists like blondes, some like reds. Maybe you love cutting short hair but are thrown off by long, curly hair.

The point is, the perfect client is different for everyone.

So let's rephrase the question. Now ask yourself this. What is *your* perfect client? To me, the perfect client is one that is a joy to be around, comes in every four to six weeks, books appointments a year out, refers *all* of their family and friends, buys whatever product you recommend, and trusts you completely.

In my book, that's a pretty perfect client to have. The problem is, those "perfect" clients are quite elusive and hard to find. But they do exist. You just have to know where to look.

Let's brainstorm for a minute. What type of person do you want sitting in your chair? What kinds of clothes do they wear, how old are they, how do they talk, are they edgy or conservative? Are they men or women? Do they have short or long hair? Blonde, brown, red or black?

Maybe you haven't thought about these things before, and that's okay. Most of us are so excited to have *anyone* sitting in our chair at first. However, now is the time to decide what type of clients you want your salon to attract. It's your business and you want to enjoy what you do, right? So why waste your time and energy servicing clients that drain your life-force? If you've been in this business for more than a day, you know what type of person I'm referring to.

What I want you to do now is picture your favorite clients. They are the ones you see on your schedule and a smile comes to your face. They are the ones you are actually excited to go to work and see. Now ask yourself why they are a favorite? Is it their great attitude? Is their hair easy to work with? Is it their friendly personality that you love to be around? Think about this. Why do you love having them as a client?

Something about them makes you feel special, right? Well, my goal in this section, is to give you ideas on how to attract more of the want and less of the don't. Ideally, we want all of our clients to be our favorites. That would make working feel a lot less like, well, work.

Taking on new clients is a great thing, but it can also be exhausting. You have probably already figured out that it's impossible to please every person that walks into your salon, so why stress yourself out by always having to be "interviewed" by the new client in your chair. They are watching you, determining if you are a good fit for them. Whether or not they come back is *their* decision. That's stressful.

I'd much rather see the same faces, time and time again. You build trust, comfortability, and rapport. Your regulars love you. That's why they're regulars. Seeing them is stress-free, which is a good way to spend your time. There are plenty of things in life to be stressed out about so let's not add something else to the mix.

So how do you find these clients? Good question. Let me tell you how I got mine. I call it the "Expert Approach".

THE EXPERT APPROACH

People often admire my clientele and wish they could attract such a loyal following. My clients are young, fun and extremely pleasant to be around. They trust my judgment and allow me to color their hair in whatever way I see fit, because they know I always have their best interest at heart. They are one reason I really love what I do.

Ever since I started doing hair, I was always drawn toward blondes. I loved highlighting, and coloring blonde hair. The fragile texture that often accompanies blondes, was something I looked forward to getting my hands into. I also liked blondes because they hated seeing roots. They were certain to be regular clients!

It's not by accident that more than 90% of the women that sit in my chair are young professionals in their early thirties with manufactured blonde hair. That's because I've engineered it that way. I built my "perfect" clientele, in less than two years, and you can too.

What if I told you that you could not only fill your books, but do it quickly, and with the customers you always dreamed you'd have? You might be pretty excited, right? Well, keep reading because I'm going to teach you how.

Of course, I didn't build my clientele like one would build robots. I also didn't spend thousands on marketing. I discovered a way to attract the type of clientele I wanted to service for less than $75.

The Expert Approach goes like this. Say curly hair is your speciality. You have it, you love it, and you know how to cut it. If all the clients that sat in your chair for the rest of your career had curly hair, you would be one satisfied camper. That would make you happy if that was your thing, right? Plus, if you love curly hair, I'm sure that means you're good at it. You might even call yourself an "expert", right?

Well, you should. If you know more than the person sitting in your chair, consider yourself an expert, because you are. You don't need to compare yourself with Guy Tang, Vidal Sassoon, or some other industry master. Just because you may not be recognized as one of the best in the business doesn't mean, for one second, that you are not an expert at what you do. You went to school, you've taken classes, and read books on the subject. As far as your clients are concerned, you *are* an expert in your field. That's exactly why they are paying to see you.

Now it's time to promote yourself as an expert. I'm sure you've taken the time to create professional business cards, right? Now it's time to print some more. Except this time, under your name or wherever you typically label yourself as "hairstylist" or "colorsit"—change it to whatever your specialty service is such as "Curly Hair Expert", "Balayage Specialist", or "Blonde Specialist." These are your *Expert* cards.

Suddenly you've separated yourself from the pack. You are no longer just an ordinary hairdresser. You can't be grouped with *all* other hairstylist's anymore.

If your goal is to have clientele full of curly-haired clients, do you think having Curly Hair Expert on your card might separate you from the pack? Absolutely! These cards are not designed to replace your "generic" business cards, only to supplement it. Making this minor (yet major) change on your business card is a big step in attracting your perfect clientele. Make sure you always keep a few of each version with you at all times.

Now it's time to take action.

Taking action is what will separate you from every other stylist trying to make a living at it. You've already demonstrated that you're willing to learn and try new things to succeed. You're reading this instead of watching tv or partying with your friends. You care to do what others don't want to. You understand that this is a cut-throat business and that in order to get ahead, you have to work for it and take risks.

Say you're out running errands or shopping at the mall with the girls. Suddenly, out of nowhere, you see a woman walk by with the most amazing hair. You think how great it would be if every one of your clients had hair like that! She's your ideal client.

But instead of letting this moment pass, view it as an opportunity. Instead of wishing she was your client, why not invite her to be your client. Remember, you have your special cards, which is your golden ticket. You are not just anyone anymore.

Let's imagine that your prospect has beautiful, curly hair and you have declared yourself as a "Curly Hair Expert", as stated on your speciality business cards.

Walk up to her, politely grab her attention, and hand her your card with a smile. Tell her you really love her hair, and if there's anything you can ever do to help, to please let you know. She will probably smile back and say "Thank you."

It's absolutely fine to just smile and walk away at that point. You did it! There's no need to hang out and create awkward conversation.

So what did this accomplish then?

One, you offered them an amazing compliment. Who doesn't like compliments, especially about their hair. And two, you showed that person that you care about your work, that you're personable and a go-getter. It doesn't matter if you happened to be shaking with nerves at the moment, which may happen at first. Most everyone will be flattered and appreciate your effort and bravery.

Here's the magic moment. Once you walk away and your curly hair prospect looks down at the card you just handed her, she'll notice you're not just any hairstylist. You're a "Curly Hair Expert". Ooh la la!

If I had curly hair, I'd know how special it really was. I'd also understand how difficult it can be to get a good cut and color. I would *only* want to go to someone that knows what they're doing. Not just any run-of-the-mill hairstylist. I would want a Curly Hair Expert. Wouldn't you?

The chances that you get contacted by that person in the future has just skyrocketed exponentially. Good work!

Now, let's pretend that you hate working with curly hair as a stylist, and you wish your entire client base was made up of blondes. Personally, that was my goal, so as you can imagine my business cards read *Blonde Expert*.

That's when I took to the streets. Utilizing the same strategy that I offered to you, I'd walk up to my perfect clients, compliment them on their hair, and confidently hand them my card.

I was extremely nervous at first, as I'm sure most of you will be. That's alright and understandable. Any time a person puts themselves out there, it can be uncomfortable. What if I trip on the way or slur my words? Who cares. You don't know them. Just accept that you will be awkward at first and move on. The success and happiness of your business depends on it.

As I became better at it, and less concerned on what I looked like, I was meeting new people and having entire conversations with them, like we'd known each other for years. At times, I'd even find myself giving hair consultations on the sidewalk, and even setting up appointments!

After I'd been at it for a short time—beating the streets as I like to call it—my phone was ringing like you wouldn't believe. Best of all, it was *my* perfect clients that were calling.

Just like that, my days were soon filled with my favorite type of client. Who says you can't pick your clients?

So what type of hair are you passionate about? What are you excited to work with? Short hair? Men? Fantasy colors or natural? Blondes, brunettes, redheads? Picture for a second what your ideal client looks like. How do they talk, dress, and carry themselves. Remember, you don't only want the hair, you want to attract the person too. In order for us to be truly successful in our profession, we have to enjoy who we spend our days with.

Make your new "expert" business cards and get started. Don't sit around your salon gossiping and complaining that you don't have enough clients. Your success is your responsibility. Get out of your comfort zone, meet some perfect people, and make success your reality.

Instead of waiting for them to come to you, go to them. Find out where your clients work and play, and find ways to get in the door.

Here are a couple other ways I attracted my ideal clientele that you might be interested in implementing yourself.

GO GREEK

If you live in an area that has colleges and universities, this could be a good source of getting hair in your chair. I never like the idea of discounting services, but I do believe in offering different "special rates", to fraternities and sororities in the Greek system.

For example, one marketing campaign I ran (which worked wonders!) was a Sorority "Rush to the Salon" Special. For me, this proved to be a great way to get college-aged, social media savvy girls in the salon, a couple times a year.

I also specially targeted sororities that I found to be predominantly blonde, as that is my speciality.

Greek *Rush* happens a couple times a year, usually right before both Fall and Spring Semester. For those of you unfamiliar with Greek life, it's a time of year when sororities and fraternities aim to recruit undergraduate students to join their prospective Greek organizations.

Having been a part of the Greek system myself, I understand how serious the recruitment process can be. Choosing the wrong people can seriously impact your organization's reputation. As college as that sounds, it's a big deal at the time.

Sororities take it to the next level. They play the game to ensure they have the cream of the crop. Their desire to attract the perfect "sisters" is vital. To be the best they can be during Rush Week, it's imperative that they look their best from head-to- toe. They even have to adhere to a very specific set of standards set forth by their Chapter President, or they could face penalties.

Their clothes, nails, makeup, and hair, have to be on point at all times. This is your chance to become their hair God.

If you need clients in your chair, this is a great opportunity to offer a "Rush to the Salon" special. I offered it twice a year for the entire month leading up to Rush Week.

If this idea interests you, I suggest you contact the president within each sorority (there could be several on campus) and ask to speak to them about your upcoming "Rush Specials". Everyone likes special rates. If they invite you to introduce yourself and your special offer, take full advantage.

You'll need to prepare a quick, professional, yet cunning introduction about yourself and what makes you great. Make them like you. During your speech at the sorority house, offer a raffle for a complimentary service. It not only gets a new client in your chair, albeit for a comped service, but also gets you contact information to offer them specials in the future. What you're doing, is trying to attract and retain clientele.

For the raffle, pass around a sheet of paper. Everyone in attendance writes down their name and email address. I used college ruled paper so it makes it easier to cut into thin tickets, which, later you toss into a bowl.

When it comes time for your raffle, mix up the tickets in your bowl and pick a winner.

If you really want to create excitement and get more free marketing out of it, announce the raffle online and have someone video you choosing the number. Hopefully, the winner of the complimentary service will be so thrilled to have won, she'll share the video over her vast network of friends. Some of which could be your future clients.

If you do choose to do a video to announce your raffle, be sure to post it onto your social media platforms, such as Instagram and Facebook. Yoe can ask that next to their name and email address, that they also add their instagram handle which makes it easier for you to share the video with the winning ticket holder.

Pro-Tip: The reason why we ask for email addresses is to add them to our contact list. They will automatically be contacted whenever you send salon news, updates, and promotions, holiday specials, or other special offers.

If you are located in a higher price point area, you may only see these clients a couple times a year, as college kids don't usually have the time or money to see you on a regular schedule.

They can, however, serve as great marketers. Having grown up in a socially connected society, they are masters of social media and many have a vast reach of social influence. So make sure you give a lasting impression because your masterful work has the potential to get posted and reposted all over social media.

Whenever you can, let other people do the marketing for you. It's received better and doesn't cost a thing.

The same technique could be applied to fraternities if men's hair is your niche. Offer your services at a "special rate"—not a discounted rate—for the span of a few weeks, a couple times a year, during Greek Rush.

PREFERRED BUSINESS PARTNERSHIP

Another marketing idea that worked wonders for me, is with other small and local, service-industry businesses. I'm talking about family-owned restaurants, unique coffee shops, or boutique clothing stores. Places that still employ a fair amount of staff but aren't connected to the bureaucracy and red tape of a large corporate entity.

I put together a 5X7 flyer—something nice and colorful that would hopefully be placed on a break room cork board, for all the prospective employees to see. This flyer noted a special relationship with my salon (which was my brand), offering a *Preferred Business Partnership* special rate incentive to receive hair services. Each company that participated in this program would then be able to offer their staff promotional rates of 25% off the ticket price for the majority of my services.

You may think that restaurant owners might not go for something like this. But, why not? They love it! They are able to offer their employees a generous discount to a local business, without having to pay anything out themselves. It's a win-win.

To make my business sound more official, I even included an elegant letter, along with my flyer, and gave it to the restaurant owner myself. The letter stated that they were selected, in a non-salesy way, to be part of a *Small Business Incentive Program*, which helped support neighboring businesses in the area.

Neither party can go wrong. If you're trying to get clients in your chair, this is another strategy that is only going to benefit you, and will only cost you the price of the ink to print the flyers.

When I got started, I picked five of my favorite restaurants and retail stores near my salon. I made sure that each of these businesses had at least ten employees to make it worthwhile. Once you've pinpointed your target businesses, stop in and find out when the owner works so you can introduce yourself. You're a people person, remember? Be your fun, kind self and tell them how much you love their place. That's one reason you chose it. Be honest and sincere as you explain your *Preferred Partnership Program* and how it can be mutually beneficial. Only good can come from it.

STEP 4—WIN THE YELP GAME

"A good reputation is more valuable than money."
—*Publilius Syrus*

Online review systems, like Yelp, can be finicky beasts. A good review can be your best friend, while a negative review can crush your business.

It doesn't matter if you're choosing a book on Amazon.com or picking a restaurant for a date. The more stars something has, the more attractive it is. People associate things with higher ratings as "being better." Whether it's concerning a book or a restaurant, (or a hairdresser), it doesn't matter. What the population perceives, so shall they believe. That perception is all you should be concerned about at this point.

When a company like Yelp is on your side, (i.e., you have a favorable rating), your phone can ring off the hook with new clients fighting to get an appointment with you. Plus, it doesn't cost a thing and could prove to be your business's lifeblood, continually serving as an endless source of free marketing. All of that can be yours, *if* you have a good star-rating.

Whether or not a business's reputation is well-received online, may seem like a dice throw. It may seem like luck to have a nearly flawless, favorable reputation.

Fortunately for you, I disagree. It's not luck. It's a game. Better yet, it's a game you can win. And even better than that, I'll soon describe, in detail, how my proven strategy will help you to dominate it. It doesn't matter whether you only have one client or a thousand.

I continue to use Yelp because it is a recognizable company, and probably the largest online business review site in the US. However, I have a true love-hate relationship with it.

On one hand, I love Yelp because we haven't had to pay for marketing in over three years due to our stellar 5-star reputation. Yet, on the other hand, I hate it because getting bad reviews stink. Unfortunately, they do happen. There is nothing fun about being bashed publicly. It's a true ego-assassin. You may not have even done anything wrong, but that doesn't matter. That terrible review is online now for all to see, and there's nothing you can do about it.

It's obvious now that the game has changed over the past decade. We all used to rely on our friend's recommendations when choosing a restaurant, dentist, or mechanic. Not anymore. We'd rather Google it on our own and find what best suits our individuality. In essence, word of mouth is dying. Although it is still deemed as the most preferred referral source of all, it is a quickly diminishing source. The less people rely on their friends recommendations, the more your online reputation can decide your ultimate fate.

Whether you're just starting a salon or have owned one for twenty years, it's vital to know what the public is saying about you. Good or bad, it's critically important to always focus on strengthening your brand. Successful businesses need high-ratings, and a plethora of them, to continually stay successful.

My salon happens to be located in a city that's flooded with competition. There are over ninety salons within a five-mile radius. Now that's a lot of competing salons, but I'm not worried at the moment. That's because my salon is currently the highest ranked hair salon in my area, and has been for some time. When someone Google searches for a place to get their hair done nearby, we are always one of the first to be called.

Due to the strength of our Yelp reputation, we *never* have a slow season. In fact, we have a waitlist of new clients begging to get in.

At this point you might be wondering how you can possibly become one of the highest-ranked salons in your area, especially when other businesses have been around so much longer. Sure, your competitors may have a head start, but that doesn't mean you won't soon lead the pack. Now, although my strategy won't make you successful overnight (I don't know anything that will), it will work and you'll reap countless rewards in the years ahead. I did it myself and now I'm able to pay myself thousands more dollars per month that I don't have to spend on advertising.

One thing I've learned with Yelp is that upset people are exponentially much more likely to post a negative review after having a lousy experience. Whatever happened, in their mind, ruined their day. They feel like it's their duty, to humanity, to splash your guts all over the internet, so other people won't have to suffer similar consequences.

Again, whether or not the negative review was justified, it's still a negative reflection on the business. It's going to happen from time to time, so just accept it. Sooner or later you'll see that dreaded one-star pop up. It's inevitable. Just understand, no matter how hard you try, you can't please everyone. As long as you've put your best foot forward, you've done all you could. If someone is unhappy with you or your service, there's little you can do to change their mind.

Instead of wasting any time thinking about the naysayers, what you should be focusing on are your supporters, your *happy* clients. It's these clients, your cheerleaders, that will boost your reputation to the top.

The problem you'll face is that they *are* happy. It might not sound like a problem, but it is. Getting a happy, satisfied client to write something nice about you online, is like pulling teeth. You can ask them politely and repeatedly to recommend your business online, but they've forgotten all about you by the time they get home. That's because they're satisfied customers. Although they voiced they would "love" to write you a review, it isn't a priority in their lives.

Your job is to make it their priority, because it's a priority for you. Remember, you are a salesperson first, and this is a sale you have to make. The success of your business depends on it.

I was able to become one of the highest rated salons in San Diego, in less than three years, by using simple strategies. I haven't had to pay a dime in marketing expenses and my phone continually rings with new clients wanting to get on my waitlist.

If you're serious about your business, you need to take initiative. Our salon makes it a mission to get our satisfied clients to post raving reviews about us online, not just to boost our overall ranking, but also because the more positive reviews we have, the less impact the negative ones will make.

Here are three strategies I've personally used to build an unbeatable Yelp reputation and keep the phone ringing with new clients dying to get in.

YOUR PAST CLIENTS

For those of you not completely new to hair, this is the where I would start. It's the easiest and least stressful way to build up your online reputation and boost your client list.

First, I'd recommend reaching out to your past clients and friends. Anyone and everyone you can think of on whom you performed some kind of hair service. It could be anything from a bang trim to a full highlight. They could be your best friend or an old client from ten years ago. Anyone that can testify to your integrity and professionalism as a hairstylist.

I sat down with a piece of paper and scrolled through the contact list on my phone, jotting down the names of everyone that I had previously performed a salon service on. Then I pulled up Facebook and did the same thing with my "friends" list.

When I had my list complete, I was shocked at how many people I could contact. I called, texted, emailed and Facebook messaged them all with a nice little note, asking for support, and a hyperlink directly to my Yelp listing. I wanted to make it as simple as possible for them.

I tailored each message personally to each contact.

For instance, when reaching out to past clients, this is what I wrote:

Hi Kim!

I hope you, your family and your business is going well! Last year I finally started my own salon business and have been very successful in building a strong brand thus far. One of my biggest sources of new business is from my 5-star Yelp reputation. I know it's been awhile since I've done your hair but I was hoping you might be able to take a few moments to jot down a few nice things about myself, my skills and/or customer service on my business's Yelp page. This would be awesome! The link to my business is: [insert the link here] Your favorable recommendation would make my day. Thank you so much and I look forward to seeing you in the salon again soon!

-Ryan

My goal was simply to reach out to people that I had worked on, that liked me and would support me. Sometimes it worked, sometimes it didn't. But the 'sometimes it worked" group was all that mattered to me.

YOUR CURRENT CLIENTS

The next area I would focus on would be your existing clients. These are ones that come to you regularly for services and always appear to leave happy.

In our heads, we think getting these clients to recommend us online will be easy, right? How hard is it to take two minutes, log onto Yelp and post something positive to help your hairdresser grow his business?

Well, people, I'm hear to tell you, it's harder than you think. Much. That's because they are happy with your service, like we touched on earlier.

This is when you have to start playing the salesman.

An old marketing principle says it takes six to eight touches to make a sale. A "touch" is a contact to your prospect. In this case, your happy client. We are trying to make a sale, which means posting a positive review about their experience with you. We are asking them to write a few sentences about how awesome you are at what you do.

Now it's time to grab another pad of paper and make a list of all your existing "happy" clients. You may have already asked some for reviews in the past, but unless they've written one (or openly voiced that they won't for some reason—maybe they don't want to set up an account), then they need to be on that list.

Next, make eight columns to the side of their names, and number the column headers from 1–8. This is where you are going to notate your contacts, either by phone call, text, email, or Facebook message.

Once you have this completed, it's time to start contacting every name on that list. Each time you send a message or make a phone call (asking for their recommendation), make a check mark in the column, note the type of communication and the date at which you sent it. For instance, if you are contacting someone for the first time by email, simply write "email 4/14/16".

It's important to try to different forms of communication to reach them. Not everyone checks email, but maybe a text will do the trick, or vice versa. It's also important to record the date there as well, so that you are able to space out the communication and not annoy your clients. Our goal is to get their recommendation, not irritate them.

You know your clients better than anyone else, so maybe you should send an email once a week, and then a text three weeks later. Don't wait too long in between contacts, but also be careful of sending them back to back. You will learn as you go what works best. The point is, that you're actually doing it systematically.

Personally, I made it into a game. I made beautiful spreadsheets with fancy colors. Every time I pulled up my Yelp account and saw a shiny new review, a smile would come over my face and I could happily scratch their names off the list.

Sometimes it would only take one contact. Other times it would take eight. Sometimes it never happened, so I'd eventually stop. Not everyone wants to review and that's fine. Most will, though, and they just need a little nudge.

Don't worry. As long as you continue to be a nice person and do your job well, they will continue to come to you and love you all the same.

EXCHANGE SERVICES FOR REVIEWS

When I first started out on my own, a few years back, I literally only had about five paying clients. Not nearly enough income to survive on. Not by a long shot. I needed clients in my chair and I needed them fast. I also needed to begin building a strong online reputation, so that when someone looked my salon up on Yelp, they'd be impressed.

It was time to be proactive. It was time to leave my comfort zone and hit the streets. When I was at the salon and didn't have clients, which was 95% of the time, I'd grab my business cards and take it to the streets. I would walk around the neighborhood and search for my "perfect" clients. When I found someone with hair I'd like to work with, I'd simply introduce myself as a master stylist that was new to the area. I'd then offer to do their hair, whether it was cut or color, in exchange for a positive Yelp review if they were satisfied with the service.

I've never asked someone to give a fake or fictitious review because I feel that most people can see right through that. So perform the service, win them over, and they will be more than happy to rave about their wonderful experience.

This is a win-win method to build your reputation. First of all, your new customer is getting a professional hair service for free. Chances are they will be very satisfied as long as you can deliver a better than average service. They may even refer their friends to you—paying customers! This is a also a perfect opportunity to pre-book their next appointment at the regular price. Also, in the off chance they don't take a liking to the finished result, the chances that they will write you a negative review is slim to none, even if you totally destroyed their hair. You gave them a free service after all. They might even tip you!

STEP 5—THE PRE-CONSULTATION

"Before anything else, preparation is the key to success."
—*Alexander Graham Bell*

One day, about three years ago, as I was walking into work, I realized I was practically hyperventilating. The strange thing was, I had no reason. I had a full schedule, I was booked out about a month and had new clients begging to get an appointment with me. This was about a year before I created my newest venture, Salon Spruce. I caught my breath and then tried to understand why I felt this way. I was a success. I should be extremely happy, right? But, instead, I felt lost, lonely and afraid of what my day would bring.

I was averaging at least two or three new clients daily, because my reputation in and around San Diego was top notch. Everyone wanted an appointment with me. If you searched best hairstylist in San Diego, I was always one of the first names to appear at the top of an organic search. I didn't understand. I was killing it. I was pulling in more money than I had ever dreamed, and I was only booth renting.

Then it occurred to me. Every day I was walking into the unknown. As much fun as it was to have new clients, I never knew what to expect. Each day brought a new challenge, but the challenge wasn't always good. I was doing all of the booking on my own through an online booking system. Sometimes new clients would call and I would make the appointment, but more often than not, they were utilizing the online booking system. This is great technology, but it can bite you in the behind. I'll tell you why.

Great as it is to automate this process, most people requesting a color appointment, for example, really have no idea what to book for themselves or what to schedule. This leads to clients mis-booking their appointments all the time. It's impossible to set aside enough time for each client when you have no idea what it's going to take. If you've been in the hairstyling business for more than a few months, you already know that not every service is black and white. There is a lot of grey area. Not everyone has perfect hair. In fact, most of my clients, new and existing, fall into the "color correction" category.

This is no fault to the client. How are they supposed to know the difference between balayage and a foil highlight? I had new clients scheduling a root touch-up, when what they really needed was a full head of highlights. In their defense, it *is* a root touch up. They want more highlights because their hair has grown out. It's just a root touch up that requires two to three hours instead of one.

If you are double-booking, which I was, this causes a major problem. It only takes me twenty minutes to apply color to roots, whereas a full-highlight may take over an hour. This can quickly throw your entire day off, and enrage clients that may have to wait, or come back another time for the service they thought they had already scheduled.

Something like this was happening to me every day. So instead of being excited to meet new clients and create gorgeous hair, I was putting out fires and angering people. This needed to stop immediately if I was to maintain my sanity and keep pressing on.

After careful thought, I decided I'd had enough. No more walking into the unknown. No more crossing my fingers and hoping for a smooth day. I decided it was time to take steps to set myself up for success, each and every day.

SET YOURSELF UP FOR SUCCESS

How was I going to do this? Simple. From that point forward, I would require that all *new* clients, requesting a color service, come in for a consultation. Not your typical consultation that you *should* have every time *any* client sits in your chair before a service. A pre-consultation: a ten to fifteen minute chat about what the client wants, was needed before scheduling the color service. This will serve several purposes:

- **Determine which service to schedule.** Is it a highlight, balayage, or root-touch up? Is it all three?
- **Determine how much time to book.** This is important for you to know if you are double-booking, and important for the client to know what to expect.
- **Set realistic expectations.** Does the client have ten years of black, box color on her hair, and want to go bleach blonde in one visit? This is when you can explain the steps it will take, and if it is even possible.
- **Test the hair.** More than likely you have had clients that thought they could walk into CVS, grab a box color from the shelf, and recreate celebrity hair color from the comfort of their bathroom. In your experience, how has this turned out more times than not? Dreadful, of course, which is why they are sitting in your chair.
- **Decide if you *want* this client.** Your reputation and your brand are everything. That being said, if you are not confident you can meet the client's expectations, it is your right to refuse service. Let someone else mess it up. You don't want *your* name tarnished. I've personally refused to work on clients that have unrealistic expectations.
- **It shows commitment and builds trust.** If a client is willing to show up for ten minutes, days in advance of their color appointment, they are serious about their hair. That's the kind of client you want in your salon.
- **It protects you.** Use this opportunity to *secure* their appointment time by holding it with a credit card. We have a 24-hour cancellation policy that states if you cancel (or no-show) an appointment within 24-hours of your scheduled appoint-

ment time, you will be charged a percentage of the scheduled service. To this day, we have never had to put this into effect, because they always show up, or cancel before the 24-hours. This is insurance for you and your time and prevents no-shows.

STEP 6—THE FOLLOW-UP

"Start by doing what's necessary, then do what's possible, and suddenly you are doing the impossible."
—*Publilius Syrus*

What I'm about to tell you is one of the most important magic bullets in this book. I believe it has been one of the biggest keys to our success and ongoing 5-Star reputation. We all know that a huge factor in building a name for ourselves stems from consistently delivering fantastic results with each and every client.

However, following up with our clients after their service is equally as important. In my own business, it's effect has been instrumental in our quick growth and massive success. That's because there is a strategy to it. Although it's one of the easiest and most effortless things to do, sadly, most hairstylists and salons alike simply don't do it.

I've never had a follow up from a salon or a hairstylist and I've been to a lot over the years. What about you? Ever received a personalized follow up from a salon receptionist or hairstylist? If so, how did it feel? Pretty good, right?

Following up with a client is definitely not a new, grand idea. Many businesses already have it in place as a part of their daily practice. Think about the last time you called your phone company to chat about your bill or to switch your phone plan. You probably received a computerized, follow up phone call asking if you'd be willing to take a quick survey to rate your customer service experience. Even though you probably just hang up, like I do, you get a follow up.

The same goes for other service providers. I recently went to a doctor because I was sick. A few days later, the receptionist called me to check in on how I was feeling. That was nice, I thought. I'll definitely go there again because of that extra touch of service.

So why don't salons and independent stylists do it regularly? Maybe they think it doesn't matter. Maybe it's because it's just one more thing to keep track of. Or maybe they're afraid of what they may hear. Our artist egos are fragile things. When someone says they're unhappy with our service, it's hurts a little. Sometimes a lot. Maybe we avoid following up with our clients because we don't want to hear that we weren't perfect.

I think the biggest reason we don't follow up with our clients is because when they left the salon happy, we assume that they are happy. Haven't you heard before that you should never assume anything? Nothing different here. Just because they were in love with their hair when they left, doesn't me they are the next day when they don't have a professional styling it. That's when your client might notice that one side is a little longer or that one highlight is bolder than the rest. But you'll never know that if you assume they are always satisfied.

I've been following up with my clients since the first month I got into the hair business. To me, it just seemed like a nice thing to do, and I wanted to ensure that I was doing a satisfactory job.

I still remember the very first follow-up phone call. I was working at a high-end salon in Walnut Creek, California, and was eager to build my business as fast as possible. I knew that the best way to create traffic and build a reputation for myself was to deliver high quality work and boost my referral business. This was important to do because I worked at a big salon and walk-ins were distributed fairly and amongst all of the stylists, so building a business would take time.

We didn't have social media and texting wasn't a thing yet, so if we wanted to build our business, we had to do it the old-fashioned way; meeting people and asking for referrals.

I knew I had to find a way to get people to tell their friends about me. One way to do that, I thought, was to follow-up with my clients about a day or two after their cut or color and make sure they liked my service. If they did, I would politely ask them to refer me to a friend.

In this case, my new client was male and came in for a haircut. Nothing fancy, but at this salon even simple services cost a pretty penny. During his service, I made sure to be at my best. I cut his hair to the best of my ability, offered great customer service, thanked him, and escorted him to the front desk to check out. He seemed happy when he left, but as I said, never assume anything.

The next day I gave him a quick courtesy call in the afternoon. I told him that I was the hairstylist that cut his hair the previous day and that I was following up with him to make sure he liked his haircut. How do you think he responded? Exactly. He was shocked. He had never received a courtesy follow-up call for something as simple as a routine haircut. I could even feel him blushing on the other end of the line because he felt so cared for.

He graciously thanked me and told me that what I was doing was a great thing. He mentioned that I should keep doing this because no one else did. He indicated that he would start doing it in his own business because of the impact he felt. And all it took was a thirty second phone call.

Needless to say, not only did he become a client for life, he immediately referred several friends and family.

From that point forward, I made it part of my daily routine to check in with my new clients. What I came to find out later in my career, now more than twelve years later, was that this habit and this simple act does a lot more than just show clients that you care.

WHY YOU SHOULD FOLLOW UP

1. Ensures customer satisfaction. Just because this is obvious, doesn't mean that salons do it. Checking in with clients after their service is a great way to determine whether what you are doing is working. Are you giving a good haircut or color service? Are your clients happy with the way the salon runs? Is there anything you can do to improve your client's visit and make it more enjoyable, professional, and memorable?

2. Be memorable. By taking the time out of your daily schedule to check in, it lets people know that they are not just a number, but a person that you'd like to have back in your salon. Compare it to writing a letter to your grandparents or giving someone a birthday card. It's a simple gesture that means the world to the person receiving it, and can quickly show that you truly care because you went the extra mile.

3. Avoid negative reviews. Do you remember the last time you had a bad experience at a restaurant, a car dealership, or a coffee shop? I'm sure you do. I bet you also told everyone you know and maybe even complained about it on Facebook. Maybe even wrote a nasty review about the business on Yelp. I bet you also did it within two days of having that awful experience because it was still fresh in your mind.

This is why we insist on following up within two days. If a client is unhappy with a service, the sooner you can find out, the better. For example, say you follow up and they tell you they didn't like the cut. This is when you apologize that the service didn't meet their expectations and that you'd be happy to "adjust" the cut asap. (Never say "fix" because that implies you made a mistake). Same goes for color or any other service. You need to find out what they were unhappy about and adjust it, or else their bad experience about *your* service may go viral across social media.

4. Boost positive reviews. Just as quickly as a client's bad experience can put a ding in your reputation, someone's great experience might go unannounced.

Why is this? Because people love to complain. We all know this. However, when you pay for a service and you are satisfied with what you got, you're a happy camper. You may even be ecstatic about your experience, but are you necessarily going to rush home and post a 5-star review on Yelp? Probably not, unless that's your thing. Most happy people just continue on with their day.

This is when the follow up helps you. When you find out that your client is 100% satisfied, now is your opportunity to pounce. Ask your happy client to take two minutes and say something nice about you and the service they received. This "follow up" is your chance.

They still may or may not do it, but it never hurts to ask. Casually remind them each time they come in. Sooner or later they'll feel so badly that they haven't done it yet, they might even do it during their visit.

Keep asking. It works.

HOW TO FOLLOW UP

Just as there is an art to coloring hair, there is an art to following up. It should be done the same way, every time, with each and every client. This will ensure consistency and take the guesswork out of it so that you don't have to recreate the wheel every time. It also needs to be personal. Nothing computer generated. We make it a practice to follow up with every new client within 48 hours after their service. Anything past that is useless. That's because after a couple of days your client has already made up their mind whether to love you or hate you and there's nothing you can do about it at that point.

Our follow-ups are personal, prompt and specific, and we do it via text message. It couldn't be easier. Most people today don't answer the phone, so why should we call? That's why we text. Plus, statistics are on our side. More people respond to texts than phone calls. They will also be more honest with you since there is less chance of rejection.

In the case of clients that still have landlines, we will follow up that way but that's not many anymore. Our goal is to not send an email or one-way conversation. We want honest feedback. We need to know how their experience was from beginning to end, and if they feel satisfied.

Our follow up text says something like this:

Hi Claire,

Thank you for recently coming in to Salon Spruce! Just a courtesy follow-up :) How are you liking your new hair?

-Jeni from Salon Spruce

This is the start of every follow-up text conversation and it has worked for years. I'd recommend using this simple text, with the punctuation exactly as it appears. It is personable, professional, and straight to the point. It also makes it easy for the client to return a candid and honest response.

Also, be sure to end the text by stating who it's from. Since "Jeni" does nearly all of our texting, it looks like:

[message]

-Jeni from Salon Spruce

Please note exactly how this dialogue is written, especially the wording, sentence structure, and punctuation. It may seem like a minor detail to you, but trust me, it works for a reason. How you say something, can either make you look like a trustworthy professional or an unreliable amateur.

A word of warning. Not everyone will respond saying they love their hair. That's okay. This is your opportunity to "adjust it more to their liking." Just make sure not to get defensive, angry, or tell a client they're wrong. That is a game you will not win. Instead, suck it up. You are not perfect. Nobody is. Accept it, move on and continue to follow up for the sake of your growing business. It's worth the occasional humbling experience.

STEP 7—ASKING FOR HELP

"Hiring the best is your most important task."
—Steve Jobs

If you've been consistently applying the principles and strategies carefully laid out for you in this book, I'm certain success will begin to find you soon enough, if it hasn't already. As your business ultimately grows, so will your client roster. Your phone will ring more and your schedule will fill up. Be prepared, because when it happens, it spreads like wildfire. Soon your clients will be booking two or three appointments ahead, just to make sure they get their favorite Saturday spot.

Although having your books filled up and your phone ringing off the hook is a good problem to have, it definitely comes with its own challenges. With all this new business banging on your door, you undoubtedly will become increasingly overwhelmed. Your time will become more limited, you'll be ruined by exhaustion after work, and you won't have an ounce of energy left to continue to send your follow up texts or update your social media accounts. Even your customer service will falter, all because you are now too busy.

Again, this is a good problem! Remember, not long ago you had less than five clients and weren't sure how you were going to pay rent. Now you have money flying through the door. We all started from scratch and nobody wants to go back there.

Again, lots of business is a good thing. But how do you deal with it? How do you maintain your energy and a high level of customer service with each and every client?

Easy! You get some help.

There are a couple of options. You could hire a manager. Hmmm, expensive. What about an assistant? Yes, that's a possibility but then you may find yourself responsible for payroll taxes, and trust me, that's expensive, especially in California. Plus, you just started making real money but maybe you're not ready to jump the gun and have an employee. Well, how about recruiting the help of a family member or "remote" assistant, which is what I did in the beginning.

When I first opened my salon suite, my wife, Jeni—fiancé at the time—offered to help me out in her spare time. She was busy as a professional horse trainer, and was only able to help out a few hours a week. I took what I could get. Plus, I wasn't making enough money to hire full-time professional help. Jeni helped me return emails, respond to texts, book my clients, and occasionally answered the phone. Remember, I have a separate cell phone strictly for business purposes, which I was able to leave with her during those times she was able to help me out. She could work remotely and didn't have to be at the salon.

Jeni isn't a hairstylist nor ever wants to be. That's besides the point though, because I didn't need another hairstylist. I needed a manager, and thankfully that is one of her strong suits. She can manage and organize anything you put in front of her so that anyone can understand it.

Her few hours of help per week made all of the difference in the world.

Now that you're busy, you need to ask for help. Forget hiring someone. Do that later when you can afford it. For now, though, ask a family member or a friend. Someone you love and trust. A person with your best interest at heart.

With Jeni helping me, I couldn't go wrong. She's someone I can always rely on because my success is *our* success.

Is there someone you love and trust that would be willing to offer a little bit of time each week to help you with your newfound business? If it's a family member, take them out to dinner every now and then. If it's a friend, kick them a few dollars off the books.

Regardless, find someone you trust to help out for just a little while until you can afford to hire someone full time.

Don't forget, your talents lie in hairstyling. Try not to stray from that. The majority of your time should be spent focusing on creating beautiful hair, not answering the phone, filing taxes, rescheduling clients, and ordering inventory. That is not your expertise. Let someone else worry about that.

As my business rapidly expanded, not only was I finally able to hire an assistant, I was also making enough money so that Jeni could quit her job and work for our salon full-time as our Social Media Strategist/ Operations Manager.

I understand that not everyone is lucky enough to have a boyfriend, girlfriend, or spouse that is willing and able to contribute their time to help build your brand for free. I get that, but as I mentioned, you only need someone to start helping out a few hours a week. Beg if you have to. That's all. Just get the ball rolling.

Plus, if you've gotten so busy now that you need help, you're probably making some decent money. Think about hiring a friend. Although you may not be ready to pay for a full-time assistant or manager, pay someone part-time and allow them to work from home. Teach them how to return texts, schedule appointments, and answer the phone. This doesn't have to be rocket science. Just get someone to help you do the day-to-day so you can focus on the client in your chair. Trust me. This will help you maintain both your sanity and exemplary customer service.

Here are some key reasons why you need to ask for help at this stage in your business:

1. Managing and Organizational Tasks. Most of us as stylists are artists first and business people second. That's okay. We are usually good at one or the other. Since our main goal on a daily basis is to offer our clients the best service we can provide during their visit, that's where our focus should be, at least 90% of the time.

It's time to think about having someone else take over the daily tasks of answering the phone, posting on social media, booking appointments, and doing your follow-ups. Once you're booked solid, ten hours a day, you won't have the time or energy to manage or organize. Your energy and customer service needs to remain high. Focus on what you know and love—hair—and recruit someone else to run the business side of your salon.

2. Maintain a High Level of Customer Service. I still remember how it felt when the dominoes started to fall. My phone was dinging with newly scheduled appointments thanks to my online booking service, my days were filled with new clients, and my reputation on Yelp was soaring. I was thrilled and had a new energy about me. I did it!

And then the fatigue and exhaustion hit me. I was working ten to twelve hour days, five or six days a week. I was answering the phone, returning phone calls, scheduling, and rescheduling clients during the few breaks I'd have during the day while my clients were processing. Running late for my next client became a regular occurrence. I wasn't doing my follow-ups anymore and my social media posts had stopped. Soon enough I realized I had lost my personal touch. I wasn't giving my clients the best because I didn't have the energy. I knew something had to change if I was going to maintain my sanity and get back to offering my clients the very best in customer service.

Finding the right help makes all the difference in the world. When you can afford an assistant, get one. When you can't, ask a friend or a loved one to help take some pressure off your shoulders. Anything helps. Trust me. Stick to your guns and be sure to consistently deliver the exemplary customer service that brought your new clients here in the first place.

3. Make Your Brand Appear Bigger Than It Is. Appearances are everything. The bigger your brand appears, the better it makes you look. It doesn't matter if you're running a single person salon suite. If you have other people working for you (or helping out) on the outside, those are your people. They don't need to be physically in the salon to be part of your team.

Oftentimes, I may be the only one working in my salon suite. But if you ask me about my team, I'll tell you. I have Jeni (my wife) running the show behind the scenes. She's our salon's Operations Manager and Social Media Marketer. I have an assistant that helps me out during the week when I'm double-booked. I have a graphic artist and lighting guy that I've used in the past and can use again when I need something. I'll even mention my product reps. They might not be directly on my payroll but they'll help me to succeed in any way they can because they want to keep my account.

Do you see where I'm going with this? You probably already have a team and you didn't even know it. Any person or company that you pay or helps your business out, is part of your team. Now, doesn't that sound awesome?

You are building a brand one step at a time, and when that time has come to recruit help, even if you are working alone all day long in a small suite, you need to let people know who's working behind the scenes. You're growing your team. Be proud of it. Post photos on your website with biographies. You are a business, not an individual anymore. Refer back to the chapter on "Act Like a Business". This is your chance to let people know that you are not just a hair stylist. You are an artist, entrepreneur, and salon owner, and now you are forming your competition-crushing team.

You can't call a doctor's office and speak to a doctor right away, can you? This shouldn't be any different. You're a hair doctor. The more professional you are, the bigger your business looks from the outside.

4. Get the Truth From Follow-Ups. An unhappy client won't always tell their stylist when their service expectations have not been met. It's awkward and feelings can be hurt.

However, this same unhappy client will feel much more comfortable telling a salon manager or receptionist. For instance, if you have someone like Jeni doing your follow-ups, I guarantee you are more likely to get a truthful response than if you were directly texting the client yourself.

In this business, it's vital that we get the truth about how we are doing as professionals. If you have unhappy clients, you need to know about it. Only then can you address the issue and "adjust" the problem in whatever way you see fit.

ABOUT THE AUTHOR

Ryan Weeden owner and operator of one of the highest-rated salons in San Diego (Salon Spruce), is founder of Masters of Balayage (an advanced balayage-color training company), an educator for the world-renowned Kevin.Murphy Brand, a Celebrity Stylist, and is the Author of the Suite Success Series. His work has been featured in several magazines. He speaks at events and demonstrates advanced hair color techniques as an independent educator and stage artist.

Ryan is a talented professional, friendly and engaging, who proudly accepts the responsibility of creating a memorable experience for his clients. Yet, it only takes one visit to realize there is much more to him than meets the eye.

Although he may call the East Coast his original home, he has always been a Southern California kid at heart, having spent much of his childhood listening to the Beach Boys and daydreaming of epic surf. A born entrepreneur, Ryan has always felt most alive when he is creating something. He didn't find himself in the artistic hair world until he had tried his luck on the stage and screen as an actor in New York City.

He decided that the acting life, in an overcrowded metropolis, wasn't his cup of tea. It took only the simple suggestion of a trusted friend's mother that made him pursue a career as a hairdresser.

Ryan, an alumni of The University of California, Santa Barbara, received his early hairdressing education from two of the world's most prestigious companies, Toni & Guy Hairdressing and Redken.

He currently resides in a beautiful home, just a block from the beach in sunny San Diego, with his wife Jeni, their dog Abbie, and horse, Finnegan.

Made in the USA
Columbia, SC
24 November 2018